Made in Poetry

Ekta Somera

Made in Poetry

ISBN 978-0-620-93281-3 Printed in the Republic of South Africa.

Copyright © Ekta Somera 2021

There is a poem screeching against the glass walls of my throat. Nobody can hear it trying to escape the threshold of my heart, *but it is there.*

"Ekta's writing is a collection of all your favourite flowers in one garden. This is certainly a masterpiece filled with nothing but motion and thought-provoking words."

- Mhlengi Classic Mafu(Author of Dear Woman'dla)

"A young, bruised and eminently strong heart runs through the pages of this debut eruption of a volcano of evocative poetry and lyrical prose. This is what it is like to shatter into pieces and then, with careful deliberation, recreate your truth with golden adhesive. The Japanese call it Kintsugi, Ekta presents you with the beautiful mosaic that she is."

- Parul Gahlot (Hoarder of poetry and writer of myriad articles)

"Ekta Somera offers a journey into her world with unrelenting sensitivity, courage and vulnerability. Allow her to entice you with captivating images, charm you with tantalising verse, then surprise you with insights of spirit that belie her tender age."

- Jack Devnarain (South African television and film actor)

"Made in Poetry" by Ekta Somera is a perfect combination of poise which both encourages and challenges one's inner soul. Ekta's skill of speaking about world issues is astounding. She manages to reign you in as she speaks about life, love, and everything in between. I found myself on a journey of self-discovery whilst reading some of the poems which hit so deep that it leaves you wanting to change – yourself, your community, and your world.

- Lynn Kerchhoff (Author of My Shack)

To those who believed in me
a handful of pages is not enough

Contents

Part One

Part Two

Part One

The Destruction

Love is as inevitable
as suffering is consequential
but empathy,
empathy grows like vines –
leeching onto our skin,
covering each mistake
in masking tape –
burying the scars we won
at the battles we lost,
to salvage the essence
of our feelings,
for kindness is a parcel
delivered by those
who have not always received it

She wore the sunlight
like an oversized sweater
and somehow
her warmth reached you
before her skin could
although when night came
her golden face would frown
at the roots that held her down
as if she longed for a breeze
to take her to some place
where darkness ceased to exist
for this yellow flower was buried
in every woe the soil carried

the sunflower

Growing up in a broken family
turns you into either
a black sheep or a lone wolf
neutral and devoid of sentiment,
you're often misunderstood by
those who haven't stood unarmed
at the centre of a warzone,
but those who have know
why disappointment became
your constant expectation,
they understand what it takes
to lose your sense of wonder
while climbing cold shoulders
in order to survive,
even when home becomes
people who hurt
you hold on so tightly
because the familiarity of pain
is what you thrive on

Longing for the stars
a trip to mars
perhaps anything with a scenery
to distract me
from the mundane things I see
when I close my eyes
and fake reality
sometimes home
isn't the best place to be

At the edge of a branch
I once slipped off,
an invisible noose
held on to the remains
of my childhood –
no better than
the shoes I wore
which never really fit –
despite the distance I walked
a gloomy cloud stalked me,
mimicking my sorrow - into a reign
of seasons that never seemed to alter
the storm which weathered
the things I felt - into paper
breached by a spark lost in the wind,
farewell – damned memories

remembrance to forget

If ever you were in the vicinity of a loner, you might believe there is tranquillity is solitude, but if ever you were a loner, you know solitude is an escape from the pandemonium in a world that never could hear you screaming.

Gold drips down the rusty bars
as crystals fill empty sockets
that gawp without any clarity
ah, tragedy –
from a deck of deception
a spade was picked to bury
my entire entity beneath
the ground I could not escape
ah tragedy –
a zoo is but a museum
for the blind to marvel
at those with sight
surviving like ornaments
glued inside a glass cage
ah, tragedy –
the blank space trapped
between in and sanity

trapped

It is dolour
that brutally obliterated
the girl I used to be
ideally, as the rose picked
to represent love
often cherished in bouquets
placed in adversity
for only thorns to remain,
I was confined to a tower
imagining all the beauty
this world contained,
labelled insane
by ordinary folk
who never could see
the roses growing
through the cracks
surrounding me

the secret

I was called a puzzle because they couldn't figure me out until, I hit the ground and my pieces fell perfectly into place after the fall, that's when they looked in awe at the mosaic mistaken for so long.

Briskly brushing my teeth
as each bristle strokes
toothpaste like white paint
glazing a blank canvas
I think back to yesterday,
you're losing it they told me
if only it were that easy
to remember

What is lost I wonder
but today must be the day
I remember where it's kept
before it's gone completely,
for twenty-one years it brewed
like a shipwreck inside a teacup
surely ruins can take a vacation

Forget the melancholic undertow
the Bermuda triangle rips into
a greater sense of freedom
for a mind as lost as mine
there are no directions I can find
nor any rules to follow –

Perhaps it's okay to drift away
sometimes they don't say,
but here's a little secret –
nothing worth talking about
started with a mind placed
in a little head all day

misplaced mind

I was often mocked to believe I could be the most peculiar person to exist, but I think now, in a world full of critically misunderstood people, there ought to be someone who feels slightly strange, odd and out of place, with a passionate rage just like me.

The wise warn the weary
of the menacing wolf
underneath sheep skin
yet only the foolish may know
to be wary of the wool
tucked beneath wolves' skin
for the unpredictable
is often more threatening

As millennials wander in wonder
wondering whether one should
be wandering in this era
like hippies trapped
in the wrong generation

The questions we're afraid to ask
hide the answers we keep searching for
nothing makes sense
this those who actually think know
for there are no wise nor foolish
it is all a maddening paradox

It takes a great deal of courage to be yourself in a world full of unnecessary rules and vile opinions, there is nothing wrong with being different. If you're brave enough to step out of the crowd and stand up for whatever you believe in, that is one hell of a victory.

On her sleeve she wore
a kind of love this world
was not prepared for
and unfortunately
it would take centuries
to understand
for she loved with a love
ten thousand years ahead of time

She was often lost in the intricacies of her own vulnerability. Fear masked her eyes as she took the fragile seal of her body, like band aids ripped from a wound. She seemed as delicate as rose petals are to a poet, but so is a grenade until it is forced to reveal what is kept inside.

Her bushy hair could never be tamed
and she was often misunderstood
the way most quiet people are
an eloquent disguise for those
who came face to face with fear
and did not close their eyes

Tears roll down her cheeks
like morning dew
on a delicate petal
as she walks toward the fire

There is something
incoherently magnificent
about a woman as frightening
as lightning who strikes
wearing fear as a strong suit

You should know
she is both
the calm and the storm

In thunderous rage or plunging ecstasy sometimes, a crystal ball cracks open and our portal of clarity splinters into a glistening trail of glassy shards, like the crevices upon which the moon shines, it is the tears we shed that remind us, we're made of stardust and light.

Once upon a time
she used to read love stories
by candlelight at midnight
so, she expected a fairy tale
but to her demise
the prince came disguised
as a Trojan horse
her kingdom was destroyed
and the girl who used to read
became a writer to end this story
happily ever after

Sometimes the library becomes a cemetery for all our feelings trapped within the depths of the books we read with a broken heart.

I was a museum before
you stepped in blindfolded
and broke every piece
of my heart on display
turning me into
a mosaic of mistakes

Heartbreak is pouring your heart out
to somebody who walks away
with an umbrella over theirs

Love leaves a residue. The bruises we wear like purple skies and twilight blues disappear in a few days, and the earth-shattering battle scars remind us that the clouds may float away, but the sky will always remain.

You wake up slowly and then all of a sudden, your chest weighs more than your little hands can bear, but that doesn't stop you. You might be losing a battle with your mind at war, but you don't give up. See, the world depends a lot on your strength to tackle each day.

Life happens, people miss things that will happen again. The autumn leaves dipped in honey paint the sunset in a mess of red, yellow, and orange. Most of the time we miss it, and this happens every day, that's how people miss people, they keep happening but never in the same way.

When the hope you are dependent on
begins to sail with the paper boat
taking your love away
in a flood of emotion

Watch it disappear into the horizon
as the sun revolts into the day
and newfound hope makes its way
with a love that wants to stay

You don't always realise it, but sometimes you aren't in love with a person, you're in love with the way they make you feel. That's what makes it difficult when they leave, you begin to miss the way you felt, as if nobody could make you feel that way again

The crux of a situation does not always depend on the people involved, but the feelings instead; it is possible not to like someone you once loved or call truce with a nemesis, what's difficult is believing a person is still the same. In the aftermath of change, there is consequence and perception, each time we experience sunshine or rain – it is only the weather that changes, the day is still the same.

The fickle night carried
the daunting weight of doubt
as the moonlight grazed
the lonely garden I paced
to plant the seed of gratitude
with hope beneath despair

Suddenly joy began to bloom
with love on the horizon
from that moment I knew
whatever morning dawns
would be enough
to carry one through

Wildflower
I watch you grow through the dirt
but if I turned this painting
upside down
it would look like you fall from the sky
when the stars go to hide
while the sun fades out of fear
as the people turn to night

Wildflower
I watch you glow
when they pick on your environment
while laughing at the absurdity
of flowers growing next to me
deep down I know
they admire your beauty

As tears turn into clouds
unfathomable feelings
plough through the sky
my sorrows are purged
into rain for the flowers

Birds build nests on me
as if my bare arms
are branches on a tree
I don't mind carrying them
it is far more appealing
than inviting people in
only for them to criticise
the colour of my skin
or the weight I carry
these are my walls
this is my home
and I will share it with those
who appreciate the mayhem
of the person I am

skin and bones

You have only seen a reflection of what you appear to be. Who you really are depends on the places you find yourself and the people you get lost with, not your waist size or the skin you're wrapped in. You are a construction site, a work in progress, not your disability or weakness. Hair grows outrageously and out of control, a natural disaster we tend to survive. You might feel pretty obnoxious or incongruous sometimes, individually we're all different, but together we create an exquisite bouquet of flowers.

They are all the same, but you
you are not afraid to stand out
and that is intimidating

They think you will succumb
to the fear of being odd
if you are rejected
because the cloned masses
will never understand
the freedom that comes
with being different

Take a walk down the hall
of a masquerade ball
try to befriend the faces
beneath the masked grimaces
before you could tell me
who I am or what I should be

The lion who conforms to ideals of a sheep, becomes a part of the wolves' feast. Remember this, before you could tame your mane or swallow your roar to follow their norms.

I am sorry the world tried to convince you to hide in shame, unless they could force you to fit into a place you don't belong. I am here to ask you not to change because ultimately, *love is all that matters.*

45

There are secrets we keep
at the tip of our tongue
to hide the power we possess
beneath smouldering rage
for the words we do not say
brew fire and lightning
which scare people away.

You are entitled to feelings which do not require the validation of other people. You are allowed to be angry when something doesn't go the way you expect it to. There is nothing wrong with having expectations because I know how hard it is not to. You are filled with emotions you cannot explain, do not be so hard on yourself, it is okay to feel disappointed. If you look closely, there is always something to be proud of, *you tried, you hoped, you believed,* and that takes a courageous deal of bravery.

I don't believe that words spoken out of anger are true, they are merely a result of our obnoxious thoughts at a time when we can barely think. If you want to know what a person truly feels, listen to the voice that cracks from compressed feelings.

It feels like along the way
there was something amiss
that lead me to this place
surely, I am not meant to stay
in your home when you're away

I stood at the door with grimace
wanting nothing but to run away
the lump in my throat choked me
as I tried to swallow the truth
I would never be able to digest

So, now I walk around
with an abyss stuck in my chest
since the day I accepted
death as my nemesis

the pinnacle of loss

There isn't a way to understand the pain inside of somebody else. It's easy to look at somebody and think you know what's best for them, but people aren't easy to know. The description of pain is as distorted as those who have described it.

When something breaks, you don't hide the pieces and pretend it's still whole; you can't place flowers in a broken vase. The thing is, pain is as inevitable as death, but death is the end and pain is a consequent ending.

Thinking back to some memories is like spinning sugar into candy floss, but the sweet remembrance quickly turns into tumbleweed, for some people are merely a kiss from the wind of a passing shower, that lingers for a lifetime.

I admire the sheep dogs, those who can't get all of their ducks in a row, the odd and eccentric, the looney bins, those people who are often rejected, cast aside or forgotten, the ones who admit to knowing nothing, but are always eager to know more.

52

Faith, the epitome of love
a selfless credence,
will cease to exist without
the essence of forgiveness
and the daunting absence
of fear and doubt.

The frost bit of my ears
as I steered into the looking glass
it took only a mystical gleam
of hope smeared across the slope
as I sought after a reflection
which seemed slightly familiar

Framed in crimson glazing
a caricature sneered at me and
an odd shiver slithered down my spine
as wonder sparked a pirouette
in my contemporary spirit

The snowflakes mimic the stars
this I realised as they circled my head
on the journey back to reality
after the exasperating bump –

Insanity must be madly
in love with me
for suddenly the sense of longing –
to fall in love with a mirrored display
does not feel excruciatingly lonely

a soliloquy

I admire those who aren't afraid to admit they're a little out of their head, this world is maddening after all. We're each made up of our own little tragedies; the time we wasted, the people we miss, that chance we never took, the goodbye we forgot to say. I think it takes a great deal of madness to say, to hell with it, maybe you have to be a little crazy to survive.

I have learnt that there will always be knives thrown at your back, venomous words spat to your face and sometimes the storm cloud over your head pours acid rain. I know sometimes it feels as if your life is crumbling like an apple pie in a greedy mouth, but the way I see it, you can either allow it to make you cruel, or choose to be kind.

Forgive, because you loved the only way you knew how to love and perhaps that wasn't enough, maybe it was too much, but you have to learn how to forgive so that the weight love carries, doesn't settle in your chest.

Forgiveness is an attribute of love,
when you forgive,
you become a beacon of love.

Do not expect to be happy all the time. Sometimes we have to stare into the abyss, enjoy our madness and appreciate the world for what it is. We need to explore the unknown and understand the inexplicable. Sometimes happiness creates a distortion only sadness can restore.

At the dusk of childhood,
I watched as the twilight erode
into a street of stars
no greater than shattered glass
taped to a festering sky,
oozing – as darkness reigned
from the crevice of a wound
hand stitched to conceal the rue
brewing by the hour

At the cusp of dawn
I bid farewell to the bird
drowning in the archived
sorrow beneath my ribcage
ah, child I am sorry
if only I'd said, if only I'd known
this dainty world has more
than you have seen blindfolded
don't hold your breath
there is beauty

the breach of innocence

Part Two
The Renaissance

I was dilly dallying barefoot on the grass with a dandelion in my grasp when a bee flew into my hair. I ran away in time to forget my wish, but there was this little monarch butterfly... in the moment it felt like I crept into the pages of a book, but this actually happened to me.

When someone loves you, you will know. It will feel like all the love you lost along the way has come back to you, the same thing happens when you decide to love yourself.

i am my own home and love is my centrepiece

The thing I find most fascinating about life is the essence of change. It is impossible to fit into an elaborate sentence, therefore, we should never be defined by our past or the way we are living.

Time is irreversible because some things are only meant to be felt once. Mistakes are vital in the process of being human, fortunately for us, *there is hope*, a possibility that if we are given that moment again, chances are we'll do it right.

You can start over, don't listen to them, close the doors. Your past will always be there to remind you that you are no longer the person who you once were. Open a window, a little fresh air is enough for you to realise that the possibility out there begins *within* you.

There are stories only you have to tell, because there is no one who looks at the world in the way you do. There is no one else who listens to the whispers tucked in a soft breeze or understands the wilting petals whimpering. There is no one who feels the earth in the way you do.

you are the one

There is a lifetime of stories trapped in an hourglass, instead of burying who you are beneath the sand, let a few grains slip through the cracks and allow flowers to grow. Others' may live small lives, but not you. You are a rose bouquet in a snow globe, eloquent and unique.

68

I am not proud of the person I used to be,
but what is a warrior without painful memories.

She was the girl
who bred dragons
to destroy her past
who slept with wolves
to face her fears
who worshipped phoenix
to rise from the ashes
of who she once was

resurrection

Beware of the girl
who learns from her mistakes
the one who dances with her shadow
to prove she is not alone

Beware of the girl
who wouldn't pick a diamond
over a pearl
the one who uses her sword
to save dragons
and conquer the world

When you want something with all of your heart, pick up the dagger, the sword, the bow and the arrow. If it means that much to you then fight for it, it must be yours, just don't lose hope in the battle.

Our weakness becomes a strong suit
the moment we realise that without it,
we lose our sensitivity, empathy,
understanding and appreciation,
the very essence of our entire being.

By merely looking at a person you can never tell what they're thinking, until your eyes sync and slowly, but then all of a sudden, you're carrying the weight of their world.

That is because we are not who we think we are. We are empaths, lovers, healers and everything that could never fit into a thought. We can think, but we still won't know, because we feel to understand the unknown.

When you feel like giving up sometimes, the universe connects like a dot-to-dot puzzle. You let out that sigh and a breeze carries it to the sky, whispering secretly to the clouds, but the sun listens and suddenly, the whole world is shining upon you.

In nature
there are no mirrors
yet beauty is a reflection
the moth admires the might
of its own wings as it soars
next to the butterflies
who don't think of competing
when they graciously
share pollen amongst the flowers
while the bees collect nectar
to make sweet honey

butterfly effect

Your light
illuminating from within
shines through
intimidating those
afraid of their own shadow

Fluster you must not
when those you love leave
for many are unable
to handle the exposure
but rest assured
like moths drawn to a flicker
the right people
will always surround you
because pure light
has no shadow

The wind carried a rhyme
quite out of tune
and the butterflies followed
like wildflowers
draped from the clouds
the dreamer watched from afar
trapped in a jar of caterpillars

Mocked for the way she dared
to fly before earning her wings
the caterpillars refused to believe
they could ever be as free
as petals surfing on the wind
but trapped in a jar
the dreamer taught the others
how to conceive passionate credence
for who we are is far more important
than what we appear to be

the butterfly in a jar of caterpillars

It is brave to believe in even the slightest possibility that you may have what it takes to change the world, for it is often those with the most absurd and outrageous beliefs who make all the difference.

The finest honey
glazed a copper orb
brewing like rich coffee
in the eye of the patriarchy
alas, they marvelled as she revealed
the birth of a new era

The soil sunk into the shape
of each paw stamping the trail
for the next generation to follow
the same route that brought
even the sunrise to bow in awe
when her wings first rose to flight

A gist of hope ignited a revolution
in every heart that followed
the tiger in the sky
who could lead grey scaled minds
toward the possibility of polaroids
thus, the reign of the monarch butterfly

the renaissance

Most people are born lucky, they are destined for greatness, but once in a while, ordinary people with hearts' full of hope make little wishes that come true, and suddenly the world becomes a lot more magical.

There are tiny wisps of hope tucked in quiet places everywhere, it is buried in the creases of a bedsheet and tangled in the knots of your hair, it is the whispering of a wish that sticks to your fingertips, like the taste of golden syrup, lingering in the moment after a kiss.

The bees chased
the honey bears
which followed
my scent
since that time
my lips were glazed
with a sweet taste

our first kiss

There are memories swirling inside of us, a galaxy of forget-me-nots and remember when's we share with some being, as the stars collide for our stories to entwine like constellations.

The big bang – to say the least
was how it all seemingly began,
a crush very similar
to a lemon squeeze,
from fresh petals
to fallen leaves,
gusts of wind flurried
by a fragrant breeze,
like a floral overdose amid
a galaxy of starry beings –
thus, our coexistence

constellations apart

I remember smouldering flames as raging wind carried us to the centre of the bridge we tried to burn. Whatever tragedy is made of, ours entwined. I survived your bad days, and you survived mine. Together we learnt that anything is meant to be when you want it to, because sometimes, even the clock rewinds to give the perfect match a little more time.

k. h.

I threw this love far away
because he refused to stay
for some time he was gone
but it didn't take long
before he reached my heart again
only to leave me in pain
so I let him go in vain
although I had no need to worry
for we were stuck in a loop
and this was our story

boomerang

We don't give up on things we love. We give up on things we desire. There might be a passionate similarity but ultimately, true love is a peculiar bond our stubborn heart is always willing to share.

His mischievous grin
chivalrous glare
charming sentiments
and obnoxious prose
bloom flowers
inside of me

a floral overdose

The fiddling of new fonding
a whimsical clanging
of two hearts combers
a sea of birds into the clouds
strung by a thread of silver lining
a vista of love is formed

You are my north star
a muse in every way
woven into the sky
shining for me to gauge
the strength of your twinkle
against this daunting world

Laced amongst the stars
with an alluring infinite display
constantly directing my rickety life
until you became the reason why
nothing could lead me astray

the reason

Your thoughts
could bedazzle the sky
or drown flowers in rain
but you share it with me only
for it to drive me crazy
yet it keeps me sane

You are a wish that came true
a dream I woke up to
an unexpected surprise
a miracle in disguise

You are the moment
it takes a blink to miss
but I love you
in the nick of time
enough to last forevermore

Sometimes we fall in love with someone quite the opposite of us, that doesn't mean they're the wrong person. It just means we're about to go on one heck of an adventure to understand why love is such a big deal.

94

We crash into each other
rough and passionately
like the ocean combers
before a mighty storm

I stood there
like a clay pot
brittle and empty
but he placed me at the top
of his marble coffee table
and from the garden
by hand he picked
the most beautiful
flowers for me
now we both knew
I was more than a vase
but for once I felt
like feeling appreciated

to be loved

I never knew a life so bright
I used to love the night
until he came along

His presence brought a light
his absence a daily reminder
a lingering pain
that the day must get darker
for the sun to rise again

What separates an excuse from a promise is what we keep, to make sense of reality. You are mine. You are mine because there isn't a clock to tell us how long we have until it turns into a ticking time-bomb, sometimes all we have is a moment to hold onto whatever we can before we're forced to let go.

Love is not a choice, love is a connection.
Attachment to what we love is a choice.

If you've met love at the centre of a cross road, you've probably got hit by a couple of cars speeding away from it, but after that, after that you know you're either frantically pacing across the highway to hell or skipping up the stairway to heaven, and perhaps both lead to a cliff in the end but, the only risk is not taking that fall.

What on earth makes you feel
like you are incomplete?
you are crafted from the finest stars
with a built-in imagination,
constantly time-travelling
through daydreams,
you are marvellous and magical
and curious and capable,
a natural disaster
completely human

Yellow, the colour of paint
Van Gogh ate to make him happy
such is the irony
we romanticise daily
when we love
the things that destroy us

For the day will come
when the oblivion consumes us
and all that is
becomes all that was

So, to merely embrace
all that brings us closer
to our inevitable demise
may be an essential part of life

yellow paint

The essence of art has little to do with the way it appears to be, when what it does to us balances the uncertainty of our unwavering feelings. I know this because each time we touch, you turn into poetry.

A blank canvas
is *art*
to the one
who can imagine
a portrait on it

I am not an easy person to fall in love with. If you are expecting someone who is just another brick in the wall, I am not sorry to disappoint you. I am not somebody people look at with glistening eyes that cherish masterpieces. I am graffiti on the wall, the art without a price tag, worth more the priceless art.

You can paint over me, but I will never be able to conform to what is acceptable in a blind society. I live to rebel; to destroy the standard of beauty. People do not look at me in awe, but those who look remember. I am not an easy person to fall in love with, but for art's sake, it must be hard to forget me.

There is art inside each of us; a gift to unfold. So, write if you must – paint, draw, sing, build, create – do whatever it takes, but don't hide the essence of your life story from this world; it is *the beauty we are all suffering for.*

Dear Edgar Allan Poe
I surmise you have felt
the longing to explode
into a thousand ravens
as I have before
impetuously slipping
into a curious madness

From childhood's hour
I too have not been
as others were
anchored by my heart
I sank into reality –
a shipwreck
brewing in a teacup

Alone –
a dreary twilight led
the darkness astray
sincerely as I escaped
an illustrious nevermore

Ode to Edgar Allan Poe

Ah, the poet –
what a simple word
to mask a deranged lover
bashfully painting symphonies
of silence through compositions,
some listen to the melody
others hear a brewing melancholy
nothing is ever the way it seems

Surrounded by an echo of thoughts,
seemingly bewitched fingers
entwine around a piece of graphite
tucked neatly into wood with
a sole purpose to vandalise paper

A soundless voice
traveling through sight
as unrequited love is immortalised,
years of toil and suffering –
turn into poetry – for evermore
the poets offering –
a fragile soul in return for sanity

Poetry is not about using big and exquisite words, it is about sprawling out your feelings in a way that makes people understand or run for dear life. Poetry is not about relatability; every poem is a labyrinth to either get lost in or find your way out of this world.

There is little talk
about the alchemy involved
in changing the world,
ink brewing an elixir of words –
the evanescent lead of a heart,
churned into the marvelling
outpour of gold

made in poetry

ABOUT THE AUTHOR

In her debut collection, 'Made in Poetry', Ekta Somera draws upon her personal challenges whilst growing up in South Africa and finding her voice.

In her search for true happiness, Ekta began to observe people and things, which informed her writing, culminating in a literary tapestry presented to the global village.

In this strikingly honest literary offering, Ekta invites us to experience 'Destruction and Renaissance' with her, through a powerful weaving of words and imagery, causing us to absorb each reference and experience she shares with us.

Ekta reveals her extraordinary mastery of words through imagery of nature, love, sacrifices and a unique use of poetic vignettes scattered within this canvas of lexical beauty.

Ekta lives by the words of Martin Luther King Jr. "If I cannot do great things, I can do small things in a great way."

Through this debut collection of poetry, Ekta's powerful, insightful, and inspirational poetic messages aims to reach global shores and inspire dormant muted voices to soar on the wings of poetry.

- Don Beukes (Author of 'Sic Transit Gloria Mundi', 'The Salamander Chronicles' and 'Icarus Rising')

www.ingramcontent.com/pod-product-compliance
Lightning Source LLC
Chambersburg PA
CBHW061126100726
47911CB00013B/697